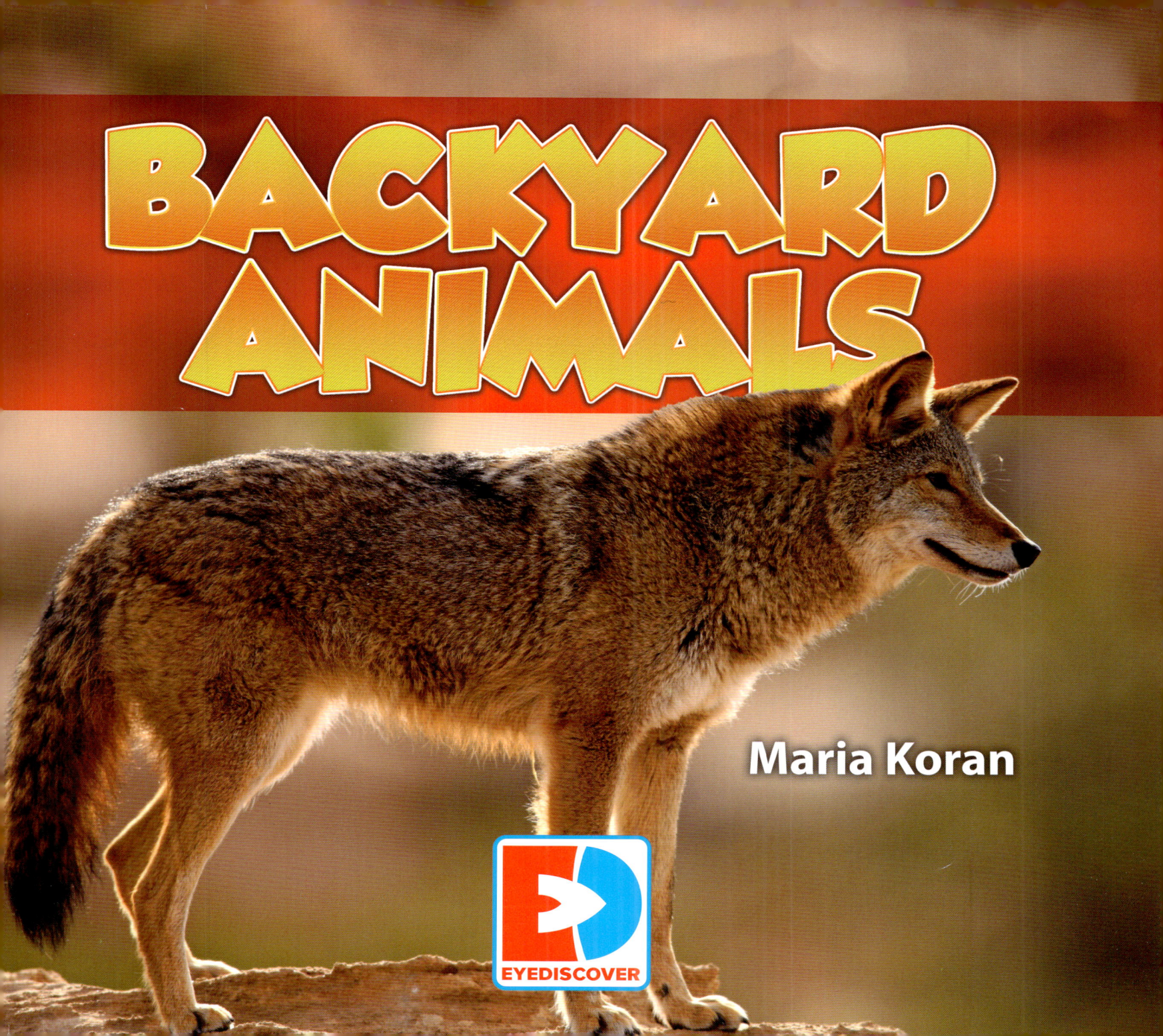

Go to **www.eyediscover.com** and enter this book's unique code.

BOOK CODE

AVP78285

EYEDISCOVER brings you optic readalongs that support active learning.

Published by AV² by Weigl
350 5th Avenue, 59th Floor New York, NY 10118
Website: www.eyediscover.com

Copyright ©2020 AV² by Weigl
All rights reserved. No part of this publication may be reproduced, stored in a retrieval system, or transmitted in any form or by any means, electronic, mechanical, photocopying, recording, or otherwise, without the prior written permission of the publisher.

Library of Congress Cataloging-in-Publication Data available on request

ISBN 978-1-7911-0770-3 (hardcover)

Printed in Guangzhou, China
1 2 3 4 5 6 7 8 9 0 23 22 21 20 19

072019
121818

Project Coordinator: John Willis
Designer: Mandy Christiansen and Ana María Vidal

Weigl acknowledges Alamy, Getty Images, iStock, and Shutterstock as the primary image suppliers for this title.

EYEDISCOVER provides enriched content, optimized for tablet use, that supplements and complements this book. EYEDISCOVER books strive to create inspired learning and engage young minds in a total learning experience.

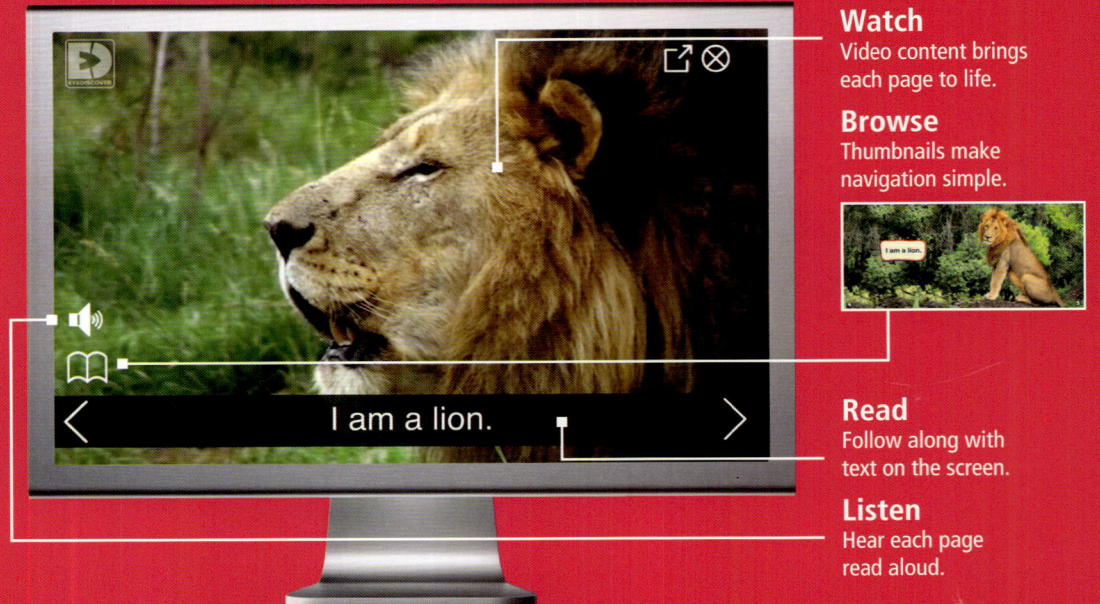

Watch
Video content brings each page to life.

Browse
Thumbnails make navigation simple.

Read
Follow along with text on the screen.

Listen
Hear each page read aloud.

Your EYEDISCOVER Optic Readalongs come alive with...

Audio
Listen to the entire book read aloud.

Video
High resolution videos turn each spread into an optic readalong.

OPTIMIZED FOR

✓ **TABLETS**

✓ **WHITEBOARDS**

✓ **COMPUTERS**

✓ **AND MUCH MORE!**

BACKYARD ANIMALS

In this book, you will learn about

- what they are
- what they look like
- what they do

and much more!

Many types of animals live near people. Sometimes, you can see them in your backyard.

5

Robins are small birds that build nests in trees. They lay bright blue eggs.

Squirrels live in holes in trees. They use holes made by birds such as woodpeckers.

Rabbits eat many different plants. Sometimes, they eat food from people's gardens.

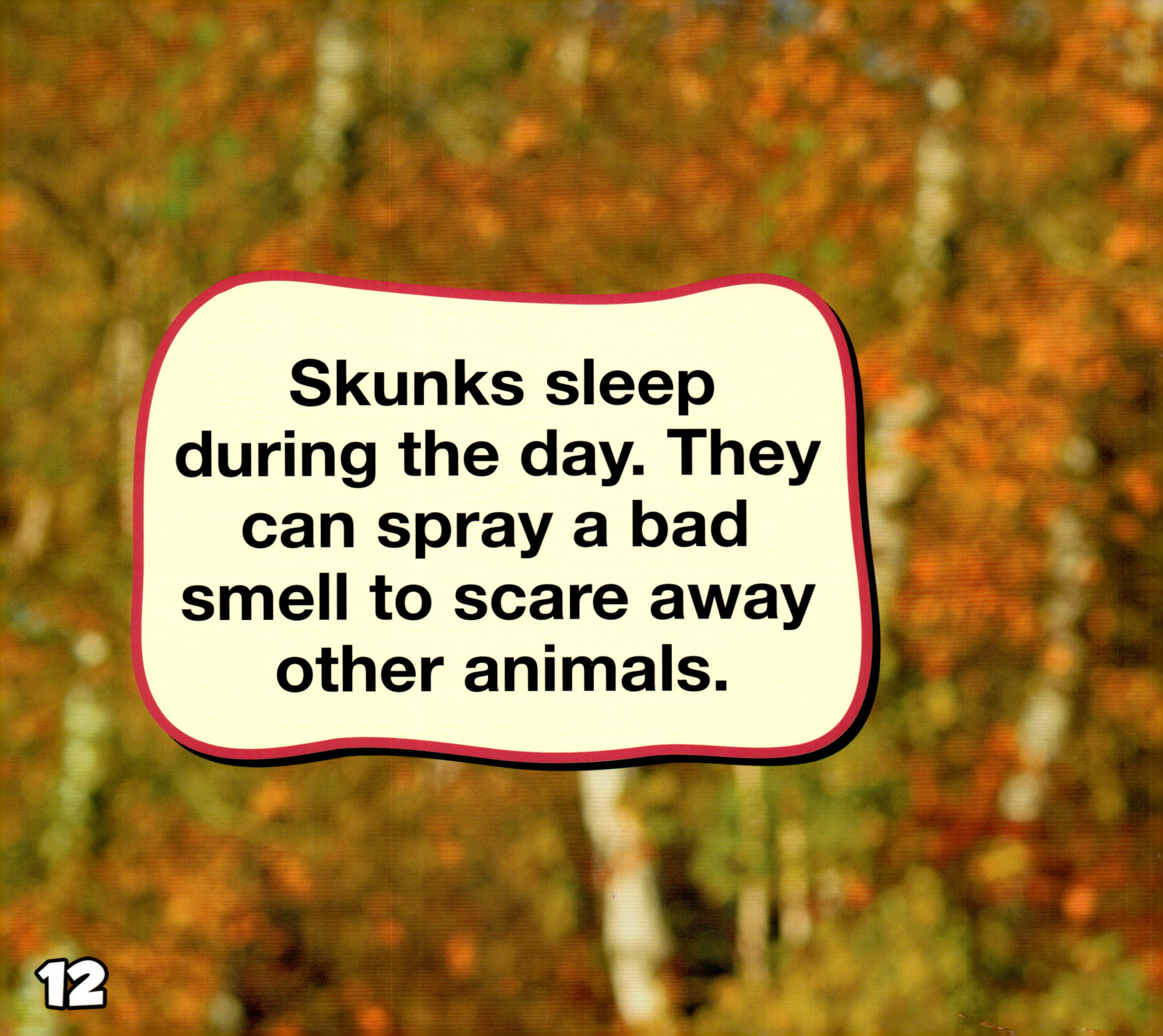

Skunks sleep during the day. They can spray a bad smell to scare away other animals.

Many raccoons live in cities and towns. They are smart and can find many different things to eat.

Beavers cut down trees to make their homes. A beaver home is called a lodge.

Many deer live on the edges of cities. They eat grass and leaves in people's yards.

Coyotes are usually shy animals. They mostly look for food at night.

BACKYARD ANIMALS BY THE NUMBERS

There are **43 different** kinds of deer.

A **raccoon** has **5** to **10** black bands on its tail.

A **coyote** can **run** at a speed of **40 miles** per hour. (64 kilometers per hour)

Beavers are the **second largest** rodents on **Earth**, after Capybaras.

A **skunk's spray** reaches about **10 feet.** (3 meters)

10 feet

American robins lay about **four to six** eggs **at a time.**

KEY WORDS

Research has shown that as much as 65 percent of all written material published in English is made up of 300 words. These 300 words cannot be taught using pictures or learned by sounding them out. They must be recognized by sight. This book contains 49 common sight words to help young readers improve their reading fluency and comprehension. This book also teaches young readers several important content words, such as proper nouns. These words are paired with pictures to aid in learning and improve understanding.

Page	Sight Words First Appearance
4	animals, can, in, live, many, near, of, people, see, sometimes, them, you, your
7	are, small, that, they, trees
8	as, by, made, such, use
11	different, eat, food, from, plants
12	a, away, day, other, the, to
15	and, find, things
16	cut, down, homes, is, make, their
19	leaves, on
20	at, for, look, night

Page	Content Words First Appearance
4	backyard
7	birds, eggs, nests, robins
8	holes, squirrels, woodpeckers
11	gardens, rabbits
12	skunks, smell
15	cities, raccoons, towns
16	beavers, lodge
19	deer, grass, yards
20	coyotes

Watch
Video content brings each page to life.

Browse
Thumbnails make navigation simple.

Read
Follow along with text on the screen.

Listen
Hear each page read aloud.

Go to www.eyediscover.com and enter this book's unique code.

BOOK CODE

AVP78285

DEC 26 2019